Gluten-Free Slow Cooker

Easy Recipes
for a
Gluten-Free Diet

by Amelia Simons

2013 by United Publishing House

Gluten-Free Slow Cooker: Easy Recipes for a Gluten Free Diet

ISBN-13: 978-1492992721
ISBN-10: 1492992720

www.UnitedPublishingHouse.com
Email: Authors@UnitedPublishingHouse.com

Printed in U.S.A

Table of Contents

Other Books by Amelia Simons

Paleolithic Slow Cooker: Simple and Healthy Gluten-Free Recipes

Paleolithic Slow Cooker Soups and Stews: Healthy Family

Gluten-Free Recipes

Going Paleo: A Quick Start Guide for a Gluten-Free Diet

4 Weeks of Fabulous Paleolithic Breakfasts

4 MORE Weeks of Fabulous Paleolithic Breakfasts

4 Weeks of Fabulous Paleolithic Lunches

4 Weeks of Fabulous Paleolithic Dinners

The Ultimate Paleolithic Collection

Introduction

With so much public awareness and research happening over the last several years dealing with the symptoms and conditions of gluten sensitivity, people are finally beginning to understand there are reasons for their bloating, cramping, and headaches after they eat. For some, symptoms like diarrhea, joint pain, eczema, and fatigue have plagued them for years without any logical explanation. Thankfully, for many, there are questions that are being answered.

Personally, I remember having severe bloating after eating meals like spaghetti, lasagna, pizza and pastries. Little did I know that the whole grains I had believed were so good for my body were actually the very things that were causing me a great deal of pain and discomfort.

Because this is a cookbook and not an exhaustive guide on how to eat gluten-free, I will assume you have a good idea of what gluten is, how it affects you, and why you need to limit or eliminate it completely from your diet. Therefore, I will not be going into any of the scientific reasons for this type of food sensitivity. There is a very good, easy-to-understand eBook you can read called, *Going Gluten Free: A Quick Start Guide for a Gluten-Free Diet* by Jennifer Wells. She does a great job of explaining topics like:

- What happens to your body when you ingest gluten

- What are symptoms to look for to see if gluten is a problem for you

- How to begin to transition from a traditional diet to a gluten-free lifestyle

- How to read product labels

- Where gluten can be found hiding in foods

- What to buy at the grocery store

- How to eat out in restaurants safely

It has been several years ago when I remember first hearing something that suggested grains were suspected of causing irritation and inflammation of a person's intestinal lining, resulting in symptoms like abdominal pain and diarrhea if they were sensitive to gluten. The speaker shared several other bites of information that caused me to seriously evaluate what I was eating and feeding to my family.

After hearing this, I decided to not eat any grains with gluten in them for a period of two weeks to see if this effort would make any difference at all in the bloating, joint pain, and feelings of fatigue I often experienced immediately after eating and in the hours and days that followed. Within four days, I felt incredibly better. The bloating had disappeared and the joint pain I had been dealing with was almost totally gone. It was then that I began to eliminate gluten from my diet and I have not looked back. Thus, began my journey of discovering how to cook and eat gluten-free.

Although I have now adapted a Paleo lifestyle (a way of eating that totally eliminates all grains), I spent several years learning about gluten-free living and developing recipes I could enjoy as well as fix for my family that were tasty and healthy. Many have asked me to share what I have learned and to offer recipes they could make—ones that would help them feel healthier and allow them to avoid the symptoms gluten was causing them to experience.

With that said, this cookbook is some of the recipes I came to enjoy as I adapted my own favorites to be gluten-free and they can all be prepared in your slow cooker! Especially in the beginning of your journey when you are trying to learn many things about how to eat without gluten, time to simply cook a healthy meal can be difficult.

Therefore, I wanted to offer you recipes you could put together for your slow cooker and spend precious moments you normally would have to use for cooking on other things.

I hope you enjoy what you will find here and know these dishes come from my heart to yours. Living gluten-free does take work, but the benefits of feeling better are incredibly worth it.

Here's to your health!

What Does It Mean to Eat Gluten-Free?

Learning to eat gluten-free is not easy, especially in the beginning. You have to constantly pay attention to the ingredients used in any type of processed foods and other products. This means you have to become a diligent label reader.

Becoming familiar with items you can eat that do not contain gluten, as well as knowing what is safe for you to consume, can be incredibly time consuming. It takes time to learn what ingredients mean and where they come from; it takes time to make substitutions for meals you like but may not be gluten-free; it takes time to go grocery shopping because you may have to shop at several different places to acquire the ingredients you need. Gluten hides in many different products so that is why you have to read your product labels carefully.

Just for fun, I have listed several food items below. Read them and vote "yes" or "no" if you think they contain gluten or not.

_____Marinades

_____Soups

_____Soy sauce

_____Rye

_____Barley

_____Modified food starch

_____Beer

_____Ramen noodles

_____Flavored potato chips

_____Couscous

_____Chicken and beef broth

_____Panko

_____Salad dressings

_____Licorice

_____Seitan

So, how did you do? If you answered, "yes" to every one of them, you would be absolutely correct! Gluten hides in interesting places does it not? And, this is by no means an exhaustive list either. It is really just the beginning of what is involved in learning about foods from a different perspective—a gluten-free perspective. This is why you have to do your homework so you can be informed about foods, what is in them, and are they safe for you to eat.

Fortunately, more and more information is becoming available to consumers like you and me from various manufacturers as they address this issue and make gluten-free products available.

If you are wondering whether or not gluten may be a problem for you, I encourage you to take this simple test. It is not an easy one, but one that could change for life as it did mine:

- Abstain from eating any gluten for 30 days to allow yourself time to see how you feel once gluten is mostly out of your bodily system

- After 30 days, eat something you know has gluten in it and see what happens and pay attention to how you feel

Like many who have shared with me, you may have experienced a complete disappearance of symptoms you thought you would always have. For the first time in your life, you may have a chance to be symptom-free.

Give yourself the opportunity to feel the best you might ever feel. If you do, you might find yourself saying as I did, "That's it! I am convinced and I am going gluten-free. I would be crazy not to!"

Slow Cooking Gluten-Free Style

Over the years, I have enjoyed experimenting and making recipes in my slow cooker gluten-free friendly. Because I am a busy wife like many of you, I can think of other things I would rather do than spend a great deal of time preparing meals in the kitchen.

Like some of you, I have accumulated several different slow cookers in various sizes. It can be a lot of fun to create a special dip and display it in a small slow cooker to keep it nice and warm throughout a party. Then there are the slow cookers that are around three quarts—just right for cooking a side dish while the big 6-quart pot is cranking out the main entrée. Sometimes it is fun to see how many different slow cookers I can have going at the same time.

While this can be fun on occasion, most of the time I find myself using my big 6-quart slow cooker. In fact, **all the recipes included in this cookbook are prepared using the 6-quart-sized slow cooker.**

Using your slow cooker for creating gluten-free meals offers the ease of cleaning up along with the simplicity of meal preparation. I will not mention this within the recipes themselves, but you can now buy slow cooker liners that fit down into your slow cooker and allow you to dispose of them once your food is cooked. These certainly make cleanup easy. Plus, you can cook some meals using foil to line the inside of your slow cooker. When the meal is done, just throw the foil away. Personally, I do not use either method because it just is not that difficult for me to clean the liners when I am done cooking. To each his own.

As you begin to get into the cooking part of this cookbook, I want to point out a few things:

1. While this cookbook focuses on gluten-free cooking, all my other cookbooks are ones you could use for a gluten-free diet. While they are written from the Paleolithic viewpoint, they include recipes without grains, helping to eliminate many gluten issues. Since I spent a great deal of time cooking gluten-free, my Paleo cookbooks and resources can be used for both ways of eating.

2. Occasionally, you may see a recipe that includes a dairy product. If you have difficulty with dairy products, then please feel free to use your favorite dairy-substitute instead.

3. If you can tolerate cheeses and you want to use some in your recipes, make sure you buy *aged* cheeses. As cheese ages, it loses lactose (milk sugar); so the older it is, the better tolerated it is by individuals.

4. If you have difficulty with butter because of the milk solids, try using clarified butter or ghee instead. This butter has had the milk solids removed. You can find places online that will even teach you how to make it yourself at home.

5. Whenever possible, buy the best food ingredients you can afford. I know money can be tight when it comes to buying organic and naturally healthy foods, but whenever you can, strive to buy the best.

6. At any point in this cookbook you see "GF," that means you should make sure the ingredient you use is "gluten free." For example, pure vanilla extract is gluten free, but imitation vanilla flavoring is NOT.

7. Whenever you use spices in your recipes, you also have to check the product label or request information from the manufacturers. Some say their pure, one ingredient spices are gluten-free, however, when they are sold in combinations with other spices, such as a poultry seasoning or pie spice combination, they do NOT guarantee they are gluten-free. You will

14

need to do some investigation to discover which companies offer gluten-free products.

8. Try to use organic and raw sugars in your cooking that are not highly processed. I use very little sugar in my cooking but when I do, I now prefer to use raw honey or coconut sugar. This is certainly NOT a requirement, but just a suggestion from someone who has been cooking and studying foods for a long time. In addition, know that in most recipes where sugar is listed, you can eliminate it if you want.

9. Making your own broths allows you to know exactly what is in them. However, if you cannot or do not want to take the time, make sure the bouillon cubes, powder, or prepared broths are gluten-free.

Slow Cooker Tips

To help you with the techniques and recipes contained in this cookbook, I thought it might be helpful to offer you a few tips on what to look for when buying a slow cooker and some general rules that apply to cooking with one.

Most all the recipes in this cookbook use a 6-quart slow cooker. There are smaller ones you can purchase that will allow you to cook side dishes while you are cooking your main entrée. In the section for "Side Dishes," you can use a smaller slow cooker, like one that is 4 quarts in size if you wish, but around here, we use 6-quart sized slow cookers for pretty much everything. Even if you end up with some leftovers, it will allow you to enjoy them later for lunch or another meal.

Slow cooking is fun, can save you money on your electric bill, simplifies dinner preparations, and cleanup is easy.

1. When you go looking to purchase a slow cooker, be sure to look for one that has a removable liner. This makes it much easier to clean. Having had ones that do not, I cannot stress how important this tip really is! However, if you already own one that does not have a removable liner, you can line

your slow cooker with a disposable slow cooker cooking bag that you can throw away so you don't have hardly any cleanup

2. For most slow cookers, the LOW setting will reach about 200 degrees F while the HIGH setting will reach 300 degrees F. Because the minimum safe temperature for cooking food is 140 degrees F, this makes slow cooking a safe alternative to oven cooking. (Be sure to check the temperature of the food you are cooking sometime to make sure your slow cooker meets these standards.)

3. Experts advise you to bring the temperature of the food you are cooking up to 140 degrees F as quickly as possible. That means, it is not advisable for you to put food that is frozen into your slow cooker. Defrost most cuts of meats and other dense food items before you place them into the slow cooker

4. As a general rule, two hours of cooking on LOW is equivalent to cooking one hour on HIGH

5. Do your best NOT to overload your slow cooker. Try not to fill it more than two-thirds of the way full to allow proper cooking of the contents

6. When cooking large cuts of meat, allow about 8 hours of cooking time when cooking on the LOW setting

7. Slow cooking can be very economical because you can use cheaper cuts of meat, yet these come out moist and tender after being cooked this way

8. Once your slow cooker is heated, try not to lift the lid because it releases a lot of the heat that has built up. It takes approximately 20 extra minutes for the slow cooker to regain the temperature it had before you lifted the lid

9. Wait to add your spices until the last hour. If you put them in at the beginning, they will lose their punch and flavor

10. One of the things I learned when adapting recipes for the slow cooker was to cut any liquids called for by one-third to one-half. Liquids do not cook out and disappear as they do on the stovetop so try cutting back on them at the start. The only exception to this would be if you are making a soup or adding wild rice to the slow cooker

11. Depending upon what you cooked in your slow cooker, they are quite easy to clean. They just take a few minutes of tender-loving care. Fill the liner with hot soapy water, or submerge it into a sink of hot soapy water. (If you slow cooker does not have a removable liner, do NOT submerge your unit). If food is stuck on, allow it to sit for 15 to 20 minutes, and then use a sponge or netted cleaning pad to loosen the baked-on food. Do not use harsh abrasive cleaners or metal scratchy pads

12. It is best to remove fats from cuts of meat and poultry before you cook them in your slow cooker

13. Something I learned a while back that might surprise you as it did me is that carrots and onions should be placed on the **bottom** of the slow cooker, *__under the meat.__* Apparently, meat cooks faster than these types of vegetables so you want them on the bottom where the heat is higher

14. Most slow cooker liners that are removable can be used safely in ovens up to 400 degrees F

15. Almost all slow cooker liners are capable of being placed in the micro-wave when the lid is removed

16. Slow cookers preserve a lot of the minerals and vitamins in your vegetables that conventional cooking does not

17. On average, most dishes are cheaper to cook in your slow cooker than they would be if you used your oven. Sometimes items cooked on the stovetop are a toss up

18. Finally, there are just some things you can't beat when using a slow cooker to make your meals – no matter what it costs to use them. Slow cookers:

- Makes tougher cuts of meat tender

- Allow you to prepare dinner in the morning, leaving you free to do other things throughout the day

- Create smells in your home during the day that are amazing!

- Give you time to take a nap and wake up to dinner fully cooked – my favorite!

Brunch Dishes

A Word about Brunch

When I was working to put together some ideas of menu choices for you, most slow cooker cookbooks contain the usual dishes for soups, stews, entrées, and even side dishes. However, when I started thinking about other meals during the day, I found myself excited about breakfast and lunch ideas for the slow cooker.

Because a slow cooker takes time before a masterpiece is created, it is not a great tool for being able to eat a tasty breakfast meal when you first get up. However, if you wake up and put together a dish for the slow cooker and turn it on, you can have a delicious brunch dish late in the morning.

These brunch recipes work terrifically for Saturday and Sunday morning brunches--days when you find yourself enjoying a more leisurely pace. This is a perfect scenario for popping a breakfast dish into your slow cooker for a few hours and enjoying it later in the morning or early afternoon.

Of course, you can always use the recipes in this section for creating tasty dishes for dinnertime. I will confess that we enjoy having breakfast meals for dinner a few times every month. Who says you have to wait for morning time to enjoy a tasty frittata?

Egg-actly Right Frittata

Frittatas are so much fun to make because there are so many things you can do and add to them that make them fun and tasty. The nice thing about them in the slow cooker is all you have to do is put all your ingredients in a big bowl, give them a stir, then pour it into the slow cooker and wait until the eggs are firm and finished cooking. A dish like this is egg-actly what you want after you have enjoyed your first cup of coffee and caught up on your emails.

Go ahead and make a batch. Frittatas keep well in the refrigerator to be enjoyed at another time. Just pop a serving in the microwave, heat, and enjoy again.

Ingredients:

- 8 eggs, beaten
- 1 onion, peeled and chopped
- 2 garlic cloves, peeled and minced
- 1 bell pepper, seeded and chopped
- 8 ounce package of fresh mushrooms, crumbled into smaller pieces
- 4 cups fresh baby spinach, packed
- ¼ cup almond milk, coconut milk, or half and half
- 1 teaspoon salt
- ½ teaspoon black pepper
- 2 cups of your favorite shredded cheese

Directions:

1. Spray the inside of your slow cooker with a nonstick cooking spray
2. Turn your slow cooker on HIGH while you get your ingredients ready
3. Using a large bowl, add the eggs and beat with a wire whisk or fork
4. Add the rest of your ingredients, but only add 1 cup of the shredded cheese
5. Mix thoroughly

6. Gently pour the mixture into your slow cooker

7. Put the lid on your slow cooker

8. Turn the temperature down to LOW and cook for 2 to 2 1/2 hours

9. Remove the lid and sprinkle the remaining 1 cup of shredded cheese on top

10. Replace the lid and cook for an additional 30 minutes

11. Check to make sure the frittata has cooked through and the cheese has melted

Makes 6 to 8 servings

Merry *CHRISTMAS* from 2014

Mr Motorhome
Home of the cleanest RV's... ANYWHERE!

South of the Border

Mexican dishes are so tasty and give you "permission" to make them as spicy or as mild as you want. This slow cooker recipe is perfect for a brunch with the girls or for Sunday after church. Just throw it in on your way out the door to the grocery store or an appointment and come home to some delicious smells. Did I mention that a dish like this is also great for dinner?

Ingredients:

- 10 eggs, beaten
- 4 cups GF tortilla chips, broken slightly (as if you got 2 or 3 pieces from each chip)
- 1 (4 ounce) can green chilies, your choice of intensity
- 1 cup shredded cheddar cheese
- 1 cup shredded pepper-jack cheese
- 1 onion, peeled and chopped
- 2 bell peppers, seeded and chopped
- 1 teaspoon salt
- ½ teaspoon black pepper
- 1 cup Half and Half (half milk/half cream), almond milk, or coconut milk

Directions:

1. Spray your slow cooker liner with a nonstick cooking spray
2. Turn your slow cooker on HIGH while you get your ingredients ready
3. Toss the tortilla chips into the slow cooker
4. In a large bowl, whisk the eggs until white and yolks are combined
5. Add the chilies, cheeses, onion, bell peppers, salt, pepper and milk to the eggs and mix thoroughly
6. Pour the mixture over the tortilla chips
7. Place the lid on your slow cooker and lower the temperature to LOW

8. Cook for 2½ hours. Check to make sure the center is firm

9. Allow to rest for 10 to 15 minutes

10. Cut or scoop servings and top with your favorite garnishes of GF salsa, avocado, sour cream, etc.

Makes 6 to 8 servings

Ham and Cheese Casserole

This is a great dish to make sometime after you have enjoyed a big ham at a family gathering. With the leftovers, you can make this delicious dish the day after or even for dinner a few days later.

Ingredients:

- 8 eggs, beaten
- 2 cups shredded cheddar cheese (your choice of mild, medium or sharp)
- 1 cup shredded pepper jack
- 2 cups ricotta cheese
- 4 cups shredded sweet potatoes or hash browns (if bought frozen, then thaw)
- 2 cups cooked ham, cubed or chopped
- 1 teaspoon of your favorite GF hot sauce
- 1 teaspoon salt
- 1 teaspoon black pepper

Directions:

1. Spray the liner of your slow cooker with a nonstick cooking spray
2. Turn your slow cooker on HIGH while you get your ingredients ready
3. In a large bowl, whip the eggs with a fork or wire whisk
4. Now add 1 cup of cheddar cheese, reserving the other cup for later
5. Add the remaining cheeses, potatoes, ham pieces, hot sauce, salt and pepper
6. Mix thoroughly to combine
7. Pour gently into the slow cooker
8. Place the lid on your slow cooker and leave it on HIGH
9. Cook for 2½ hours
10. Remove the lid and add the remaining cheddar cheese to the top of the potato casserole

11. Replace the lid and heat until cheese is completely melted

12. Check the center for doneness

13. Turn your slow cooker off when the casserole is done and allow it to rest, uncovered for 10 to 15 minutes

Makes 12 servings

Overnight Breakfast Treat

Here is a recipe you can prepare the night before so you can wake up to breakfast ready to eat. It takes a little more to prepare than some of the other recipes, but it is such a treat to wake up to, I believe you will say it is worth it.

Ingredients:

- 1 pound sausage, cooked and drained (your choice of heat)
- 1 pound bacon, cooked and crumbled into pieces
- 12 eggs, beaten
- 1 cup Half and Half (half milk/half cream), almond milk or coconut milk
- 1 onion, peeled and chopped
- 1 bell pepper, seeded and chopped
- 2 garlic cloves, peeled and minced
- ½ teaspoon dry mustard
- 4 cups shredded sweet potatoes or hash browns
- 3 cups shredded cheddar cheese or pepper jack or combination of both
- 1 teaspoon salt
- ½ teaspoon black pepper

Directions:

1. Cook your bacon, drain, and when cooled, crumble into pieces
2. Cook the sausage until it is golden brown, drain, and set aside
3. Spray the inside of your slow cooker with a nonstick cooking spray
4. Turn your slow cooker on HIGH while you get the rest of your ingredients ready
5. In a large bowl, beat the eggs with a fork or wire whisk until whites and yolks are thoroughly blended
6. Add all the remaining ingredients to the large bowl and mix thoroughly to moistened

7. Gently pour into your slow cooker

8. Place the lid on your slow cooker and lower the temperature to LOW

9. Cook overnight for 10 to 12 hours

10. Test the center of the casserole for doneness

11. Remove the lid when finished cooking and allow to set for 10 to 15 minutes

Makes 10 to 12 servings

Beef
Dishes

Yummy Beef Stew

When it starts to get chilly where I live, or I just want some good tasting beef with some vegetables surrounding it, it is time to make one of my favorite recipes. Not only is this dish flavorful, but it makes the house smell warm and inviting.

For this recipe, use some arrowroot instead of flour as a thickener and you can enjoy a gravy texture to your stew.

Ingredients:

- 2 tablespoons olive or coconut oil
- 4 pounds stew meat
- 3 large carrots, peeled and cut into chunks
- 1 large onion, chopped
- 8 ounces sliced mushrooms
- 3 cloves garlic, minced
- 1 cup GF beef broth
- 1 cup red wine vinegar
- 1 teaspoon dried marjoram
- 1½ tablespoons GF Worcestershire sauce
- 2 teaspoons salt
- 1 teaspoon pepper
- 1½ tablespoons arrowroot powder

Directions:

1. Turn your slow cooker on HIGH as you prepare the meat on the stovetop
2. In a large skillet, heat up the coconut oil OR cook the bacon pieces then drain on paper towel
3. Add the stew meat and brown the pieces on all sides in the coconut oil OR with some of the bacon grease

4. Transfer the meat pieces and the drippings in the skillet into the slow cooker

5. Add all the remaining ingredients to the slow cooker EXCEPT the coconut flour

6. Leave the temperature setting on HIGH and cook for 5 hours OR place the slow cooker on LOW and cook for 8 hours

7. A few minutes before serving, mix the arrowroot powder with a small amount of cold water to make a paste

8. Stir into the slow cooker to thicken the juices. Add more if needed

9. Serve over mashed cauliflower if desired

Makes 6 servings

Beef Stroganoff

Beef stroganoff is a great dish to make for your family. It is tasty, creamy, and goes a long way. Making this in the slow cooker will greatly simplify the traditional way of preparing this dish. Once it is done, you can serve it over rice, gluten-free pasta, or try spaghetti squash. It is a great alternative to pasta and it is good for you.

Ingredients:

- 2 pounds steak (round or sirloin tip) cut into ½ inch pieces
- 12 ounces sliced mushrooms
- 2 onions, chopped
- 3 tablespoons arrowroot powder
- ½ cup water
- 2 tablespoons GF beef bouillon or the equivalent
- 4 garlic cloves, minced
- 2 teaspoons salt
- 1 cup sour cream
- 1 tablespoon dried dill weed

Directions:

1. Turn your slow cooker on HIGH so it can preheat while you are getting your ingredients ready
2. Place the steak slices, mushrooms, and onions into the slow cooker
3. In a medium bowl, dissolve the arrowroot powder into the water, mixing with a fork until there are no lumps
4. Add the bouillon, garlic and salt and mix thoroughly
5. Add this mixture to the slow cooker
6. Cover and turn your slow cooker down to LOW and cook for 8 hours. (HIGH for 4 hours)

7. Just before serving, stir in the sour cream and dill

8. Serve over rice, GF pasta, or spaghetti squash

Makes 8 servings

Heavenly Short Ribs

I cannot think of a better way to get your house smelling great and to get your crew excited about dinnertime than with this delicious dish. It even tastes better than it smells!

Ingredients:

- 2 tablespoons olive oil
- 5 pounds beef short ribs
- 2 teaspoons kosher salt
- 1 teaspoon black pepper
- 1 large onion, chopped
- 1½ cups red wine vinegar
- 2 cups apple cider vinegar
- ⅔ cup raw honey (optional)
- 2 teaspoons Frank's Hot Sauce®
- 14 ounces tomato paste
- 1½ cups GF beef broth
- ½ cup GF Worcestershire sauce
- ½ cup GF soy sauce
- 2 teaspoons chili powder
- 5 cloves of garlic, minced

Directions:

1. Heat a large frying pan on the stovetop with the olive oil
2. Rub the salt and pepper into the ribs
3. Place the seasoned ribs into the frying pan and brown them on both sides
4. Turn on your slow cooker to HIGH to get it warmed up
5. Transfer the ribs into your slow cooker

6. Combine the remaining ingredients together in a medium bowl and mix thoroughly

7. Now pour the mixture over the ribs

8. Place the lid onto the slow cooker and cook on HIGH for 2 hours, then lower the temperature to LOW for 4 hours, OR you can cook them on LOW for 8 hours.

Makes 6 servings

Beans and Beef

Here is a recipe that has delicious taste and yet it does not require a great deal of preparation time. Green beans are one of my favorite vegetables and when cooked with the beef, they pick up the flavor of the beef broth beautifully. Feel free to use whatever cut of meat you desire—the results will be fantastic no matter what you use!

Ingredients:

- 4 pounds roast
- 3 (14.5 ounce) cans diced tomatoes, undrained
- ½ cup rice flour
- ½ teaspoon pepper
- 1½ teaspoons salt
- 2 onions, chopped or sliced
- 3 tablespoons GF molasses (optional)
- 3 garlic cloves, minced
- 1 pound bag of frozen green beans

Directions:

1. Turn your slow cooker on HIGH so it can warm up while you get your ingredients ready
2. Cut the roast in strips or slices to your liking
3. Place the meat into the slow cooker
4. Add the tomatoes, flour, pepper, salt, onions, molasses, garlic and beans
5. Stir to combine
6. Place the cover on the slow cooker and turn the temperature down to LOW for 7 to 8 hours (HIGH for 3 to 4)
7. Enjoy served over rice, gluten-free pasta or spaghetti squash

Makes 6 to 8 servings

Sweet Beef and Potato Stew

I am a big fan of sweet potatoes so I enjoy using them as side dishes and in stews and soups. This recipe lends itself to using other vegetables like butternut squash or acorn squash if you prefer, or you can even use good old white potatoes. However, the color is so much prettier when you use the others.

Ingredients:

- 3 large sweet potatoes or white potatoes, peeled and diced
- 2 large onions
- 1 teaspoon salt
- 1 teaspoon GF poultry seasoning
- ½ teaspoon black pepper
- 1 teaspoon cinnamon (optional)
- 6 garlic cloves, minced
- 4 apples, peeled and diced
- 3 pounds stew meat
- 1 cup GF beef stock

Directions:

1. Turn your slow cooker to HIGH to preheat it while getting your ingredients ready
2. Place the diced potatoes, onions, salt, poultry seasoning, pepper, and cinnamon into the slow cooker
3. Add the garlic, apple pieces, and stew meat
4. Gently pour the beef stock over the meat
5. Cover and lower the temperature to LOW and cook for 6 to 7 hours
6. The stew is done when the meat is nice and tender

Makes 6 servings

Hamburger Vegetable Stew

This has been one of my family's favorite stews for a long time. It is easy to fix on the stovetop but it is especially easy to put the ingredients into a slow cooker and let the aromas make you hungry throughout the day. Try this recipe on your crew and see what you think.

Ingredients:

- 2 tablespoons olive oil
- 2 pounds lean ground beef
- 2 onions, chopped
- 4 stalks celery, stalks
- 2 bell pepper – any color – seeded and chopped
- 2 cups fresh mushrooms
- 5 carrots peeled and sliced
- 4 cups fresh green beans, snapped into bite-sized pieces (you can also use frozen)
- 2 (15 ounce) cans tomato sauce
- 2 quarts GF beef broth
- 2 teaspoons celery seed
- 1 tablespoon kosher or sea salt
- 2 teaspoons coarse black pepper

Directions:

1. Turn your slow cooker on HIGH while you get your ingredients ready
2. Place the ground beef into a frying pan on your stovetop over medium heat
3. Brown the beef completely. Drain if desired
4. Now place the browned ground beef into the slow cooker
5. Put the onions, celery, bell peppers, and mushrooms into the frying pan and sauté for 5 minutes

6. Put the sautéed vegetables into the slow cooker

7. Put the carrots, green beans, tomato sauce, beef broth, celery seed, salt and pepper into the slow cooker

8. Stir the ingredients together

9. Cover the cooker and lower the temperature to LOW

10. Cook for 7 to 8 hours

Makes 8 servings

Poultry Dishes

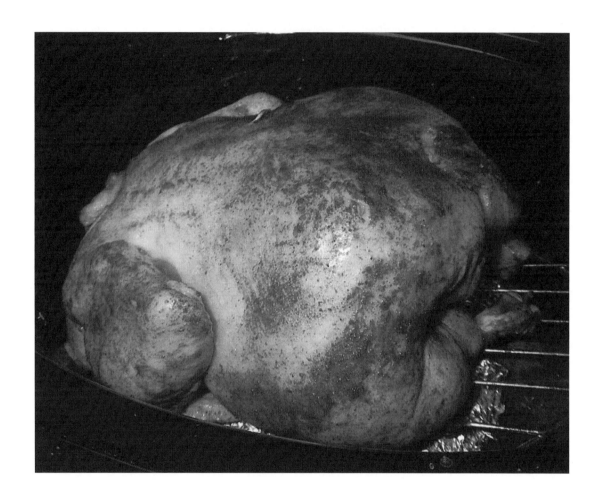

Chicken Cacciatore

Chicken Cacciatore is always a big hit around our house. The spaghetti-like sauce is delicious and the chicken comes out moist and tender.

This is so good you could almost eat it like a soup. Alternatively, serve it over gluten-free pasta, wild rice (one of my favorites) or spaghetti squash. The texture and flavors are wonderful and they fill the air of your home with beautiful smells.

Ingredients:

- 4 garlic cloves, minced
- 2 bell peppers, seeded and chopped
- 2 onions, peeled and chopped
- 8 ounce package of fresh mushrooms
- 6 boneless, skinless chicken breasts
- 14.5 ounce can diced tomatoes
- ¾ cup white cooking wine
- 1½ cups GF chicken stock
- ¼ cup tomato paste
- 2 teaspoons GF Italian seasoning
- 1 teaspoon salt
- 1 teaspoon pepper
- 3 bay leaves
- 2 tablespoons arrowroot powder
- ¼ cup water

Directions:

1. Turn your slow cooker on HIGH as you get your ingredients ready
2. Place the garlic, bell peppers, onions, and mushrooms into the slow cooker
3. Put the chicken on top of the vegetables

4. In a medium bowl, combine the tomatoes, cooking wine, stock, paste, seasoning, salt, and pepper and mix

5. Pour gently over the chicken

6. Put the bay leaves into the slow cooker

7. Place the lid on the slow cooker and lower the temperature to LOW

8. Cook for 7 to 8 hours (3 to 4 hours on HIGH)

9. Once chicken is thoroughly cooked, carefully remove it from the slow cooker

10. Make sure your slow cooker is now turned on HIGH

11. In a small bowl, whisk together the arrowroot powder and water until no lumps remain

12. Add the water mixture to the slow cooker chicken juices and mix

13. Shred the chicken and return it to the crockpot

14. Cook on HIGH for approximately 30 minutes to thicken the sauce

15. Serve over GF pasta, wild rice, brown rice, or spaghetti squash

Makes 8 servings

Turkey with Cranberries

During the holidays, I really like putting dishes together that include cranberries along with my meats, especially with turkey and chicken. Cranberries are very versatile and offer flavorful treats in your mouth. I hope you enjoy this classic combination for your slow cooker using turkey and cranberries.

Ingredients:

- 2 tablespoons olive oil or butter
- 2 onions, chopped
- 3 garlic cloves, minced
- ½ teaspoon dried thyme
- 1 teaspoon salt
- ½ teaspoon black pepper
- 2 teaspoons white or red wine vinegar
- 2 cups dried cranberries
- 2 tablespoons arrowroot powder
- 2 (14 ounce) cans whole berry cranberry sauce
- 1 turkey breast—as large as you can safely fit into your slow cooker (7 to 8 pounds)
- Remove skin

Directions:

1. Turn your slow cooker on HIGH while you get your ingredients ready
2. In a small saucepan on your stovetop over medium heat, melt the butter
3. Add the onion, garlic, thyme, salt, and pepper
4. Sauté until onions are tender
5. Add the vinegar and 1 can of cranberry sauce
6. Heat thoroughly and then remove from heat

7. In the bottom of your slow cooker, evenly distribute the dried cranberries and arrowroot powder

8. With the skin removed, place the turkey breast into your slow cooker breast side up

9. Pour the onion mixture over the turkey

10. Place the lid on your slow cooker and turn the temperature down to LOW

11. Cook on LOW for 8 to 9 hours (5 hours on HIGH)

12. Once the turkey is done, remove it from your slow cooker to a serving platter and cover it with a tent made from a piece of aluminum foil

13. While the turkey is resting, pour the juices from the slow cooker into a medium saucepan

14. Add the other can of cranberry sauce to the mixture from the slow cooker and heat through

15. Slice the turkey and use the cranberry mixture to garnish the turkey slices

Makes 12 servings

Spicy Turkey Chili

Especially around holidays, whether it is Christmas, Easter, or New Years, being creative with turkey leftovers can be challenging. Because Christmas and New Years are during cold weather in my part of the country, I created this chili recipe using turkey instead of beef. We really like this dish at our house and it is not hard to make at all.

When buying the diced tomatoes, decide how spicy you want your chili to taste. That is where the main seasonings for this chili come from and that is why this recipe is so easy—not many seasonings to add.

Ingredients:

- 4 - 5 cups turkey, cut into small cubes or shredded
- 2 large onions, peeled and chopped
- 4 garlic cloves, peeled and minced
- 3 (15 ounce) cans pinto beans, undrained
- 4 (14.5 ounce) cans Ro-Tel tomatoes or other diced tomatoes with spices, undrained
- 1 tablespoon salt
- 2 teaspoons black pepper
- 1 teaspoon cayenne pepper (optional)

Directions:

1. Turn your slow cooker on HIGH while you get your ingredients ready
2. Add all the ingredients to your slow cooker and stir to mix thoroughly
3. Place the lid on the slow cooker, turn down to LOW and cook for 5 to 6 hours
4. Top with your favorite chili garnish

Makes 8 to 10 servings

Chicken with Marinara Sauce

This recipe is so easy to make that I make it on a regular basis. It lends itself to so many options, too. You can use it as an entrée, having other side dishes with it; you can serve it over gluten-free pasta or rice (I like brown and wild rice best); or you can add vegetables to it to make it a one-pot wonder. Feel free to experiment with this one and have fun with it.

Ingredients:

- 6 fresh tomatoes, diced OR 2 (14.5 ounce) cans diced tomatoes
- 2 onions, peeled and chopped
- 2 bell peppers, seeded and diced
- 4 garlic cloves, peeled and minced
- 6 celery stalks, sliced
- 3 pounds boneless chicken breasts, skinless
- 1 regular jar of your favorite GF marinara sauce
- 2 teaspoons dried thyme
- 1 tablespoon dried basil
- Salt and pepper if desired

Directions:

1. Turn your slow cooker on HIGH while you get your ingredients ready
2. Place the tomatoes, onions, bell peppers, garlic and celery into the slow cooker
3. Place the chicken breasts on top of the vegetables
4. Now pour in the marinara sauce on top of the chicken
5. Sprinkle in the thyme and basil
6. Place the lid on your slow cooker and put the temperature on LOW
7. Cook for 6 to 7 hours

Makes 8 to 10 servings

Chicken and Rice

Chicken and rice is a classic dish that is even easier to make by using your slow cooker. Just put everything in the slow cooker, except the rice before you go off to work or spend the day out shopping, then put the rice in an hour before you want to eat. How simple is that!

Ingredients:

- 2 large onions, peeled and chopped
- 4 garlic cloves, peeled and minced
- 1 pound fresh sliced mushrooms, crumbled into smaller pieces
- 3 pounds boneless, skinless chicken breasts
- 6 cups GF chicken broth
- 1 tablespoon GF poultry seasoning
- 1 teaspoon salt
- 2 cups brown rice, uncooked

Directions:

1. Turn your slow cooker on HIGH while you get your ingredients ready
2. Place the onions, garlic, and mushroom pieces into the slow cooker
3. Put the chicken breasts on top
4. Gently pour the broth over the chicken
5. Add the poultry seasoning and salt
6. Cover and turn the temperature down to LOW
7. Cook for 6 to 7 hours
8. One hour before serving, pour the rice into the slow cooker so it is down in the juices
9. Once the rice is done, enjoy

Makes 8 to 10 servings

Chicken Taco Soup

Here is a tasty Mexican dish you and your family will enjoy. The dish is easy to make and the combination of flavors seem to explode in your mouth!

With this recipe, you can either eliminate the diced tomatoes during the cooking time in your slow cooker, or add finely diced tomatoes to your soup when you serve it.

Do not forget the chopped fresh cilantro and sliced avocados, too. They make a beautiful topping.

Ingredients:

- 5 garlic cloves, minced
- 2 onions, chopped
- 4 cups cooked chicken or turkey
- 4 cups GF chicken broth
- 2 (4 ounce) cans fire-roasted green chilies
- 2 cups of your favorite GF salsa
- 1½ tablespoons chili powder
- 6 tomatoes, diced (for the slow cooker or when serving)
- 2 teaspoons ground cumin
- 2 teaspoons sea salt
- 1 teaspoon coarse black pepper
- ½ teaspoon garlic powder
- 1 teaspoon dried oregano
- ½ teaspoon onion powder
- 1 teaspoon paprika

Directions:

1. Turn your slow cooker on HIGH while you get your ingredients ready
2. Place the garlic and onions in the bottom of your slow cooker

3. Add the chicken on top

4. Gently pour the broth over the chicken

5. Add the chilies, salsa, chili powder, and tomatoes (or wait to add the tomatoes later)

6. Cover with the lid and lower the temperature to LOW

7. Cook for 7 to 8 hours

8. About 30 minutes before serving, add all the spices and stir gently to combine

9. Serve and top with your favorite garnishes

Makes 6 to 8 servings

Chicken Fajitas

I really enjoy Mexican food and these chicken fajitas are very good. While regular flour tortillas are not gluten free, you can use some corn tortillas that say they are gluten free. With this recipe, I also like to serve it over wild rice.

Ingredients:

- 2 tablespoons olive oil (optional)
- 2 large onion, sliced and popped into rings
- 4 bell peppers, sliced into rings
- 3 pounds boneless chicken breasts
- ¾ cup GF chicken broth
- 2 tablespoons lime juice
- 2 tablespoons cumin
- 1 teaspoon salt
- 2 tablespoons chili powder

Directions:

1. Turn your slow cooker up to HIGH to get it warmed up
2. Place the olive oil in the bottom of the slow cooker
3. Put the onion rings and pepper rings on the bottom
4. Place the chicken breast pieces in next
5. Pour in the chicken broth and lime juice
6. Mix the cumin, salt, and chili powder together in a small bowl
7. Now sprinkle seasonings over the chicken
8. Place the lid on the cooker and cook on HIGH for 4 to 5 hours or turn it down to LOW and cook for 8 hours
9. When finished, serve with your favorite fajita fixings or over wild rice

Makes 6 to 8 servings

Pork
Dishes

Crocked Ham

Slow cookers make my meal preparations so convenient and keep a lot of heat out of my kitchen. Especially around holiday time or special celebrations, I really appreciate being able to put the main entrée into a slow cooker, do what I have to do, and then come back to a finished meal.

This ham recipe is like that. You put it in, stick a few spices on top, turn it on, and then when it is done, it is ready to be eaten and enjoyed.

Ingredients:

- 7 to 8 pound spiral-cut ham or whatever size you can fit into your slow cooker
- 1/3 cup honey (I like raw)
- 1/3 cup olive oil
- 1/3 cup apple cider vinegar
- 1 tablespoon ground thyme
- 1 tablespoon GF Worcestershire sauce
- 1/8 cup brown sugar, packed (or coconut sugar)

Directions:

1. Unwrap your ham and place it on a big baking sheet that has a lip to it—like a jellyroll pan
2. In a medium bowl, combine all the remaining ingredients and mix thoroughly
3. Pour and rub in this mixture all over the ham
4. Carefully place the ham inside your slow cooker
5. Cover with the lid and turn your slow cooker on HIGH for the first hour, then turn down to LOW
6. Cook for 6 to 7 hours

Serves 8 to 10

Very Berry Good Pork Roast

This pork roast is amazing! The flavor that results from the melding of these spices with the fruit makes this a treat at our house every time I make it.

Ingredients:

- 4 – 5 pound pork roast
- 2 teaspoons kosher or sea salt
- 2 teaspoons coarse black pepper
- 1 tablespoon ground cinnamon
- 1 tablespoon ground nutmeg
- 2 teaspoons ground cloves
- 2 teaspoons orange peel or zest from two oranges
- 1/3 cup pure maple syrup – grade B (optional)
- 2 pounds frozen mixed berries or just cherries

Directions:

1. Turn your slow cooker on to HIGH while you get your ingredients ready
2. Place the pork roast in the bottom of the slow cooker and season it with the salt and pepper
3. Combine the cinnamon, nutmeg, cloves, orange zest, and maple syrup and mix together
4. Pour over the meat
5. Pour the frozen berries over the meat and place the lid on top of the slow cooker
6. Cook on LOW for 10 hours
7. If you wish, you can shred the meat and stir it in with the fruit and sauce before serving

Makes 8 to 10 servings

BBQ Baby Back Ribs

I really like great tasting ribs and these definitely qualify. They fall off the bone and depending upon the BBQ sauce you use, they can be sweet or spicy. Whatever you choose, they are just downright yummy!

Ingredients:

- 2 tablespoons coarse black pepper
- 3 tablespoons kosher or sea salt
- 4 tablespoons paprika
- 2 teaspoons cayenne powder
- 1 tablespoon crushed red pepper
- 2 tablespoons garlic powder
- 2 tablespoons onion powder
- 2 racks of baby back pork ribs (they will be stacked on each other in your slow cooker)
- 2 teaspoons coconut oil
- Your favorite GF BBQ sauce (or make your own BBQ sauce--recipe next page)

Directions:

1. Turn your slow cooker on LOW while you get your ingredients ready
2. Mix the pepper, salt, paprika, cayenne, red pepper, garlic, and onion powder together in a small bowl
3. Place the rib rack out on a big cookie sheet
4. Rub the spices into the meaty side of the rack
5. Allow the rack to reach room temperature – about 45 minutes to one hour
6. Place the coconut oil in the bottom of the slow cooker
7. Cut the rack into serving-sized pieces and place inside the slow cooker. Don't worry if they overlap each other

8. Cook on LOW for 7 hours, rotating the ribs halfway through

9. After 7 hours, take your BBQ sauce and brush it on to the ribs as best you can

10. Cover and turn slow cooker to HIGH for one hour

Makes 4 servings

Homemade BBQ sauce

It can be difficult to find a barbecue sauce that is sugar free and free of additives. Try making this one. I know you will like it! We certainly do at our house.

- 1½ cups GF beef broth
- 1 small (6 ounce) can tomato paste
- 1/8 cup spicy mustard
- 4 teaspoons olive oil
- 1/8 cup apple cider vinegar
- ¼ cup GF soy sauce
- 4 garlic cloves, minced
- 1 small onions, chopped
- ¾ teaspoon paprika
- 2 tablespoons chili powder
- ½ teaspoon red pepper flakes
- 1½ teaspoons sea salt

1. Place all the ingredients into a medium saucepan with a lid over medium to low heat. You want to make sure your fire isn't too hot so the tomato paste doesn't burn

2. Cover and simmer for one hour

3. Using an immersion blender, carefully blend the ingredients so the sauce is nice and smooth

4. Cool then keep in the refrigerator

Roasted Pork with Fruit

Pork loin in the slow cooker is one of the easiest things to do. You put in the loin, add some spices and sauces, then let 'er rip! At the end of the cooking time, you are greeted with a tender and moist piece of meat that pleases the masses.

Try this combination of cranberry juice with peach preserves. If you cannot find unsweetened cranberry juice, then cut back on the brown sugar.

Ingredients:

- 2 onions, peeled and chopped
- 6 garlic cloves, minced
- 1 pound fresh mushrooms
- 1 tablespoon salt
- 2 teaspoons black pepper
- ¾ teaspoon curry powder
- 1 teaspoon ground cinnamon
- 1 tablespoon GF Italian seasoning
- ½ cup brown sugar (less if using sweetened cranberry juice)
- 1½ cups no-sugar peach preserves
- 2 cups unsweetened cranberry juice
- ½ cup balsamic vinegar
- 1 cup GF chicken broth
- 4 pound pork loin, boneless

Directions:

1. Turn your slow cooker on HIGH while you get your ingredients ready
2. Place the onions, garlic, and mushrooms in the bottom of the slow cooker
3. Sprinkle the salt, pepper, curry, cinnamon, Italian seasoning, and brown sugar on top of the vegetables

4. Next add the preserves

5. Pour in the cranberry juice, vinegar, and broth

6. Mix the ingredients together until they are well blended

7. Put the pork loin down into the mixture, rotating it so it is covered on all sides with some of the sauce

8. Put the lid on the cooker and lower to temperature down to LOW

9. Cook for 6 to 7 hours

10. Test the meat with a thermometer. If it doesn't read at least 145 degrees F (many like it to say 160 degrees), then continue to cook longer

11. To thicken the sauce: Once the pork is done, you can remove it and allow it to rest while you make a sauce using 1 tablespoon of arrowroot powder with enough water (about 1/8 to 1/4 cup) to completely dissolve it until there are no lumps. Pour the sauce into a saucepan to heat on your stovetop. Add the liquid arrowroot to the pan and heat until thickened.

Makes 8 to 10 servings

Green Beans and Ham

This one-pot meal is super simple. You can use leftover ham cut up into cubes or you can use a ham bone from a special celebration. Either way, the flavor of the ham mixed in with the green beans and any other vegetables you include, will be delicious.

Ingredients:

- 4 cups cooked ham, cut into cubes

- 2 pounds fresh or frozen green beans

- 2 onions, peeled and chopped

- 6 carrots, peeled and sliced

- 4 large potatoes, peeled and cut into cubes

- 6 cups GF chicken broth

- 1 teaspoon black pepper

- 2 teaspoons salt

Directions:

1. Turn your slow cooker on HIGH while you get your ingredients ready

2. Place the ham pieces, green beans, onions, carrots, and potatoes in the slow cooker

3. Pour the broth over the vegetables

4. Add salt and pepper if desired

5. Place the lid on the slow cooker and turn the temperature down to LOW

6. Cook for 7 to 8 hours

Makes 8 to 10 servings

Seafood and Fish Dishes

Pokey Seafood Gumbo

I grew up around the water and have fond memories of catching crab and shrimp right out of the river. My grandfather ran a restaurant so we always had some good eats growing up. I think you will really like this gumbo. It does bring back some wonderful memories.

Ingredients:

- 2 tablespoons olive oil
- 4 garlic cloves, minced
- 2 medium onions, chopped
- 3 celery stalks, sliced
- 2 bell peppers, seeded and chopped
- 2 (14 ounce) cans of diced tomatoes, undrained
- 3 cups GF chicken broth
- 2 tablespoons GF Cajun seasoning
- 2 tablespoons GF Worcestershire sauce
- 2 teaspoons kosher or sea salt
- 1 teaspoon dried thyme leaves
- 3 bay leaves
- 2 pounds raw shrimp, thawed
- 2 pounds fresh or frozen crabmeat, thawed
- 1 (10 ounce) bag frozen sliced okra, thawed

Directions:

1. Turn your slow cooker on HIGH so it can warm up while you get your ingredients ready
2. In a large frying pan on the stove, heat up the olive oil

3. Sauté the garlic, onions, celery and bell peppers until tender

4. Transfer the cooked vegetables to your slow cooker

5. Pour the diced tomatoes and the chicken broth into the slow cooker

6. Add the Cajun seasoning, Worcestershire sauce, salt, thyme, and bay leaves

7. Place the lid on the slow cooker and turn the temperature down to LOW

8. Cook on LOW for 4 hours

9. Add the shrimp, crabmeat, and okra to the cooker and cook for 1 hour longer

10. Serve over rice

Makes 6 to 8 servings

Shrimp and Rice

Here is a dish that gives you a place to use up any leftover cooked rice you might have in the refrigerator. With the addition of vibrant flavors like lemon and olives, you will feel like this dish has a Grecian flair to it. Unlike many other recipes in this cookbook, this slow cooker recipe does not take as long to cook as many of the others do. You could wait to make this one after naptime if you wanted.

Ingredients:

- 4 garlic cloves, peeled and minced
- 1/8 cup lemon juice
- 1 tablespoon olive oil
- 2 cups clam juice
- 1 tablespoon dried oregano
- 1 teaspoon black pepper
- 2 teaspoons salt
- 3 pounds large raw shrimp, peeled, tails removed, and deveined
- 4 cups cooked brown or white rice
- 6 ounce package fresh baby spinach
- ½ cup sliced green olives
- ¾ cup feta cheese
- 2 teaspoons dried parsley

Directions:

1. Turn your slow cooker to HIGH while you get your ingredients ready
2. Put the garlic, lemon juice, oil, clam juice, oregano, pepper, and salt into your slow cooker
3. Stir to blend thoroughly
4. Pour in the shrimp and stir until the shrimp are coated with the liquid

5. Place the lid on your slow cooker and turn the temperature down to LOW

6. Cook for 2 hours on LOW

7. After the shrimp are pink and fully cooked, stir in the rice

8. Place the lid back on your slow cooker and cook for an additional hour on LOW

9. A few minutes before serving, stir in the spinach, olives, cheese and parsley and mix thoroughly

Makes 8 to 10 servings

Salmon and Wild Rice

If you do not mind a little more trouble preparing this dish, you will find your efforts greatly rewarded. Wild rice takes a little while to cook, but salmon does not; therefore, it will need to be prepared differently than most of the other recipes found here. Just read the directions carefully and you will have a great tasting dish at the end of it.

Ingredients:

- 2 tablespoons butter or olive oil
- 2 cups wild rice
- 3 large leeks, trimmed and washed well, then sliced thin
- 2 teaspoons salt
- 8 cups chicken or vegetable stock
- 2 tablespoons olive oil
- 5 tablespoons GF soy sauce
- 6 garlic cloves, minced
- 1 teaspoon black pepper
- 1 teaspoon onion powder
- 8 (6 ounce) salmon fillets

Directions:

1. Turn your slow cooker on HIGH while you get your ingredients ready
2. Place the butter or olive oil in the bottom of your slow cooker
3. Next add the rice, leeks, salt, and stock
4. Stir to mix thoroughly
5. Place the lid on your slow cooker and turn the temperature down to LOW
6. Cook on LOW for approximately 4 hours
7. Once you have the rice and leeks cooking, get a medium bowl and put the olive oil, soy sauce, garlic, pepper, and onion powder in it

8. Stir to blend thoroughly. This is your marinade for the salmon

9. Place the salmon fillets in a large Ziploc bag or plastic container and pour the marinade over the fillets

10. Place the salmon in the refrigerator while the rice and leeks are cooking

11. Once 4 hours are up, lift the lid and stir the rice and leeks together. Be careful of the steam.

12. Remove the salmon fillets from the refrigerator and carefully place them on top of the rice

13. Place the lid back on your slow cooker and cook on LOW for another two hours. Discard the marinade

14. Once the salmon is cooked, carefully lift each fillet out of the slow cooker onto a serving platter

15. Stir the rice and leeks and serve with the salmon

Makes 8 servings

Soups and Stews

Hearty Ham and Vegetable Soup

I do like a good piece of ham and especially around the holidays, we seem to have plenty. Sometimes there is enough ham left over from family gatherings that I get to make a hearty bowl of ham and vegetable soup.

This recipe is yummy and warms me through and through. It is packed full of nutrition and the flavor is so good after the flavors have cooked in the slow cooker throughout the day.

Ingredients:

- 4 cups cooked ham, cut into cubes
- 2 onions, chopped
- 4 celery stalks, sliced
- 4 white or sweet potatoes, peeled and cubed
- 6 carrots, peeled and sliced
- 6 garlic cloves, peeled and minced
- 1 head of cabbage, shredded into small pieces
- 2 teaspoons salt
- 1 teaspoon black pepper
- 6 cups GF chicken broth
- 2 tablespoons arrowroot powder
- ¼ cup water

Directions:

1. Turn your slow cooker on HIGH while you get your ingredients readyPlace the ham, onions, celery, potatoes, carrots, garlic, cabbage, salt, and pepper into your slow cooker
2. Gently pour the chicken broth into the cooker and stir gently to mix
3. Cover with the lid and lower the temperature to LOW

4. Cook for 7 to 8 hours

5. If you want to thicken your soup some, turn your slow cooker up to HIGH

6. Combine the arrowroot powder with the water and stir together until there are no lumps

7. Pour this water mixture into your slow cooker and stir in until blended

8. Allow the soup to process on HIGH for 15 to 30 minutes to allow the soup to thicken

Makes 8 to 10 servings

Savory Jambalaya

This jambalaya is savory and spicy and is a wonderful comfort food for a chilly fall evening. The nice thing, too, is it is easy to put together and saves a lot of time in the kitchen from other jambalaya recipes I have made in the past. Hope you enjoy this meal as much as I have creating, and eating it!

Ingredients:

- 2 tablespoons coconut oil
- 4 bell peppers - different colors for visual appeal
- 2 onions, chopped
- 2 garlic cloves, minced
- 3 celery stalks, sliced
- 6 cups GF chicken stock
- 1 (28 ounce) can of organic diced tomatoes, undrained
- 8 ounces of uncooked chicken, diced
- 12 to 16 ounce package of spicy Andouille sausage cut into slices (try to find nitrate/hormone free)
- 2 cups okra (optional)
- 3 tablespoons GF Cajun Seasoning
- 1/4 cup of your favorite GF hot sauce
- 2 bay leaves
- 2 pounds shrimp – raw, shelled and deveined
- 3 cups cooked wild rice

Directions:

1. Turn your slow cooker on HIGH while you get your ingredients ready
2. On the stovetop in a skillet, melt the coconut oil

3. When the oil is heated, add the bell peppers, onions, garlic, and celery and sauté until tender

4. Transfer the vegetables to the slow cooker

5. Add the chicken broth, diced tomatoes with the juice, chicken, sausage, okra, Cajun seasoning, hot sauce, and bay leaves

6. Place the lid on your slow cooker and turn the temperature down to LOW

7. Cook for 6 hours

8. About 45 minutes before you want to eat, turn the slow cooker up to HIGH and put in the shrimp and wild rice

9. Stir to blend the ingredients

10. Replace the cover and cook until the shrimp are fully cooked

Makes 8 to 10 servings

Mexican Soup

Whatever time of year it is around here, we really enjoy this soup. However, when the weather gets a nip in the air, we make it even more often. This easy slow cooker meal almost seems to fix itself. Even your children can help you with this one.

Ingredients:

- 3 pounds ground beef
- 2 onions, chopped
- 2 (10 ounce) cans Ro-Tel tomatoes, undrained
- 1 (16 ounce) can kidney beans, undrained
- 1 (16 ounce) can Ranch-style beans, undrained
- 1 (16 ounce) can black beans, undrained
- 1 (16 ounce) can whole kernel corn, undrained
- 1 (16 ounce) jar picante sauce—you decide how spicy you want

Directions:

1. Turn your slow cooker on HIGH so it can warm up while you are getting your ingredients ready
2. In a large saucepan on the stove, brown the ground beef and onions
3. Drain if needed
4. Place the ground beef and onions in the slow cooker
5. Now add the cans of tomatoes, kidney beans, ranch beans, black beans, corn and picante sauce
6. Cover with the lid and turn the slow cooker down to LOW
7. Cook for 6 to 7 hours
8. Serve into bowls and top with your favorite garnishes like sour cream and shredded cheese. Also enjoyable with corn chips

Makes 8 to 10 servings

Flavorful Chicken Vegetable Soup

Chicken soup with vegetables always makes me feel good inside when I eat it, especially on a chilly fall evening. This one will give you some "kick" so beware – your nose may run faster than you! If you have small children, you may want to back down on the spices a bit, but I encourage you to try it as is.

Ingredients:

- 2 tablespoons of olive oil
- 3 - 4 boneless skinless chicken breasts
- 8 cups GF chicken broth
- 3 garlic cloves, minced
- 2 onions, chopped
- 2 bell peppers, seeded and diced
- 2 zucchini, peeled and diced
- 3 to 4 carrots, peeled and sliced
- 2 cups fresh green beans or frozen
- 2 celery stalks, sliced
- 1 teaspoon dried oregano
- 2 teaspoons chili powder
- 2 teaspoons ground coriander
- 2 teaspoons paprika
- 2 teaspoons ground cumin
- 1 tablespoon kosher or sea salt
- 2 teaspoons coarse black pepper
- 1 cup of your favorite GF salsa (you decide how hot)

Directions:

1. Turn your slow cooker on HIGH while you get your ingredients ready

2. Put the olive oil on the bottom of your slow cooker

3. Place the chicken breasts into the slow cooker

4. Add all the remaining ingredients to the slow cooker and then stir to mix thoroughly

5. Leave your slow cooker on HIGH if you desire and cook for 8 hours

6. If you wish, you can turn your slow cooker down to LOW and cook for 9 to 10 hours

7. When finished cooking, remove the chicken breasts from the cooker on to a plate and shred the meat

8. Place the shredded meat back into the cooker and mix with the other ingredients

Makes 6 to 8 servings

Meat-Free Dishes

Curried Squash Soup

Many times when I have friends over for dinner, I like to treat them to a few different courses. Whenever I serve this soup, it gets 5-star reviews. Serve this one at your next family gathering or dinner party. It is a winner.

Ingredients:

- 1 butternut squash, seeded, peeled and cut into cubes
- 2 large onions, peeled and chopped
- 4 garlic cloves, minced
- 4 celery stalks, sliced
- 2 tablespoons butter or olive oil
- 6 cups GF vegetable broth
- 1 teaspoon paprika
- ½ teaspoon coriander
- 1 teaspoon turmeric
- 2 teaspoons salt
- 1 tablespoon curry powder
- ¼ cup honey (I like to use raw honey)
- 1 teaspoon of your favorite GF hot sauce
- 1 teaspoon cumin
- 2 teaspoons ground ginger
- 1 (14 ounce) can coconut milk

Directions:

1. Turn your slow cooker on HIGH while you get your ingredients ready
2. Put the squash, onions, cloves, celery, butter, and broth into the slow cooker
3. Add in the paprika, coriander, turmeric, salt, curry powder, honey, hot sauce, cumin and ginger

4. Put the lid on the slow cooker and turn the temperature down to LOW

5. Cook for 8 hours

6. Using an immersion blender, carefully puree the soup while it remains in the slow cooker. If you don't have this type of blender, you can process it in batches using a regular blender. Be very careful because the soup is very hot at this point

7. Once you have pureed the soup, add the coconut milk and mix completely

8. Turn your slow cooker up to HIGH and allow the soup to heat through—about 30 minutes

Makes 8 servings

Vegetable Soup

I really like vegetables and because I do, sometimes I buy too many at the store. So, on occasion I will see what is in the refrigerator and make a wonderful pot of homemade vegetable soup. The best part about this recipe is the slow cooker does the work for you!

Ingredients:

- 2 onions, peeled and chopped
- 4 garlic cloves, minced
- 4 celery stalks, sliced
- 3 parsnips, peeled and cubed
- 8 carrots, peeled and sliced
- 3 large sweet potato, peeled and cubed
- 8 cups GF vegetable broth
- 2 tablespoons GF soy sauce
- 1 teaspoon of your favorite GF hot sauce
- 2 teaspoons salt
- 2 teaspoons black pepper
- 1 teaspoon thyme
- 2 tablespoons lemon juice

Directions:

1. Turn your slow cooker to HIGH so it can heat up while you are getting your ingredients ready
2. Add all the ingredients to your slow cooker and mix gently
3. Put the lid on your slow cooker and turn the temperature down to LOW
4. Cook for 8 to 9 hours
5. If you wish, you can puree the soup with an immersion blender or food processor or leave it like it is. I prefer to leave mine chunky

Makes 12 to 14 servings

Black Bean Soup

Black beans are quite tasty. Before I quit eating beans, I used to cook this soup quite often. I cannot remember how it happened, but somehow I ended up adding a little bit of orange juice to this recipe. It tasted so good that I would often surprise guests and extended family with its flavor. Hope you enjoy it, too.

For convenience, I would suggest you use canned black beans, but you can use dried beans and soak them overnight if you wish. Your choice.

Ingredients:

- 1 pound dry black beans, soaked overnight OR 3 (15 ounce) cans, undrained
- 2 onions, peeled and chopped
- 4 garlic cloves, minced
- 2 bell pepper, seeded and chopped
- 4 celery stalks, sliced
- 1 small can green chilies
- 4 carrots, peeled and sliced
- 8 cups GF vegetable broth
- 1 teaspoon paprika
- 1½ tablespoons ground cumin
- 1 tablespoon salt
- 1½ tablespoons oregano
- 2 teaspoons of your favorite GF hot sauce or more if desired
- 1 tablespoon orange zest or peel
- 1½ cups orange juice

Directions:

1. Turn your slow cooker on HIGH while you get your ingredients ready

2. Add the beans, onions, garlic, peppers, celery, chilies, carrots, and broth to the slow cooker

3. Now add in the paprika, cumin, salt, oregano, and hot sauce

4. Place the lid on the cooker and turn it down to LOW

5. Cook for 8 hours

6. Once the time has lapsed, puree the soup using an immersion blender or process in a food processor in batches. This will help to thicken the soup

7. Add in the orange peel and orange juice

8. Stir thoroughly to mix this in

9. Allow to heat through for about 30 minutes

10. Serve in bowl and top with your favorite garnish

Makes 10 to 12 servings

Side
Dishes

Spaghetti Squash

I eat a lot more spaghetti squash these days. I like it better than pasta and it is much healthier, too. Whenever I have a recipe that I used to serve over rice or noodles, I now serve it over "noodles" made from spaghetti squash. Because I use it a lot as part of my main meals, I have found it very convenient to cook it in the slow cooker. Now when my main dish is done, so is my "pasta."

Note: Early in the season, spaghetti squash has a thinner shell than when it is later in the fall. The skin becomes thicker as the season progresses so you may need to cook it a little longer on occasion. Just experiment as I do.

Ingredients:

- 1 spaghetti squash

Directions:

1. Turn your slow cooker on HIGH while you get the squash ready

2. Rinse the outside of the squash thoroughly with water

3. Place the squash inside your slow cooker

4. Leave the slow cooker on HIGH and cook for 4 hours or turn it down to LOW and cook for 7 to 8 hours

Sweet Potatoes

I really like having a sweet potato now and then but cooking them can leave a sticky mess. To help alleviate this problem, I put a piece of foil inside my slow cooker before I put the potatoes in. Then all I have to do is throw the foil away! See, I told you slow cooking was easy cleanup.

Ingredients:

- ¼ cup of water
- Number of sweet potatoes for your family

Directions:

- Pour the water into the bottom of the slow cooker
- Line your slow cooker with foil so it goes part-way up the sides of the cooker
- Turn your slow cooker on HIGH so it can warm up while you are getting your potatoes ready
- Wash the outside of the potatoes with water
- Place each potato inside the slow cooker
- Put the lid on and put the temperature on LOW
- Cook for 7 to 8 hours

Note: You can also cook white potatoes this way, too.

Spicy Carrots

This side dish is very easy to put together and offers some wonderful flavors to any main dish. Try it and see what you think.

Ingredients:

- ½ pound bacon cut into small pieces
- 2 tablespoons olive or coconut oil
- 2 onions, chopped
- 4 garlic cloves, minced
- 3 pounds carrots, sliced
- ⅓ cup spicy mustard
- ⅓ cup raw honey or pure maple syrup (I would definitely use this ingredient)
- 2 tablespoons balsamic vinegar
- ⅛ cup GF chicken broth
- 1 teaspoon ground ginger
- ¼ teaspoon cayenne pepper
- 1 teaspoon salt

Directions:

1. Turn your slow cooker on HIGH so it can warm up while you get your ingredients ready
2. In a frying pan on your stovetop, cook the bacon until done
3. Drain on a paper towel
4. Drain the grease, but leave a little to sauté the onions and garlic. Cook until tender
5. Place the carrots on the bottom of the slow cooker
6. Transfer the onions and garlic from the frying pan to the cooker
7. Sprinkle the bacon pieces on top

8. In a bowl, combine the mustard, honey, vinegar, broth, ginger, pepper, and salt and mix thoroughly

9. Pour the liquid gently over the carrots

10. Place the lid on the cooker and lower the temperature to LOW

11. Cook for 7 hours

Makes 6 to 8 servings

Cauliflower "Rice"

Cauliflower is a vegetable that is eaten a great deal around our house. Whether it is raw with a dip or steamed with broccoli, I am always experimenting. Here is a side dish of cauliflower I think you will enjoy, plus it cooks right along with any main dish in another slow cooker.

Ingredients:

- 1 large head of cauliflower
- 3 cups of GF chicken broth
- 3 garlic cloves, minced
- 1 teaspoon onion powder
- ½ teaspoon kosher or sea salt
- ½ teaspoon pepper
- 2 tablespoons chives

Directions:

1. Turn your slow cooker on HIGH while you get your ingredients ready
2. Wash and break the cauliflower head into pieces and place in the cooker
3. Add the broth, garlic, onion powder, salt, and pepper to the cooker
4. Place the lid on the cooker and continue to cook on HIGH for 3 hours or turn the cooker down to LOW for 6 hours
5. Carefully pour off as much broth as you can
6. Using a stick blender, process the cauliflower until you get the texture and consistency you desire
7. Use as the rice for some of your main entrées

Makes 6 servings

Broccoli with Almonds

I am so thankful my family likes broccoli because there are so many different ways you can fix it. It works well in the slow cooker and offers many flavor combinations.

This one is easy to prepare and is packed full of lemon and garlic flavors. Try this alongside your favorite entrée that is cooking in your other big slow cooker!

Ingredients:

- 8 individual bunches of broccoli—florets only
- 2 cups sliced almonds
- 12 garlic cloves, peeled and left whole
- 3 tablespoons olive oil or coconut oil
- ½ cup lemon juice or juice of 4 lemons
- 1 teaspoon salt
- 1 teaspoon black pepper

Directions:

1. Turn your slow cooker on HIGH while you get your ingredients ready
2. Remove the florets from the broccoli stems and place in the slow cooker
3. Sprinkle the almonds over the broccoli
4. Now add the garlic cloves
5. In a small bowl, combine the oil, lemon juice, salt and pepper and mix
6. Drizzle over the broccoli
7. Place the lid on your slow cooker and turn the temperature down to LOW
8. Cook for 5 to 6 hours or until the broccoli is done the way you like it

Makes 6 to 8 servings

Slow Cooker
Breads

A Quick Note about Gluten-Free Breads

Yes, I know that quick breads are not usually cooked in a slow cooker, but you can if you do not want a hot kitchen and you know a few tricks.

I do not know about you, but sometimes I like a good piece of bread or muffin with my cup of coffee or with my meals.

Because I am so used to cooking without grains, these quick bread recipes are from my Paleolithic diet slow cooker cookbooks. This means these recipes are guaranteed to be gluten free. If you have problems with dairy or do not eat sugar of any kind, you may want to find other gluten-free recipes you are comfortable baking. The process is still the same—the ingredients are just different.

This section includes numerous recipes that have become some of my favorites and can be cooked in your slow cooker using a bread loaf pan. **Please note: you will need to use a 6-quart oblong slow cooker in order to fit most bread pans inside.**

If you would rather not cook your quick breads in your slow cooker, you can always make these recipes in muffin pans in your oven. As with most recipes, the oven temperatures would be 350 degrees F and would bake for 20 to 30 minutes.

Before you attempt baking in your slow cooker, I want to walk you through the process so you will know how to do it. Once you learn it, you can make just about any muffin or sweet bread recipe you want.

1. Because regular muffin pans will not fit inside a slow cooker, you will have to cook these recipes in a loaf pan that fits inside your slow cooker. **Be sure to test to see if your loaf pan fits inside your slow cooker before you start!** Most 6-quart oblong slow cookers will hold a regular bread pan (8½ x 4½).

2. You will want to form four small balls made out of foil to elevate your loaf pan off the bottom of your slow cooker. If you have a small rack that fits in the bottom of your slow cooker, you can use that instead.

3. Be sure to spray your bread pan with a nonstick cooking spray or grease it with coconut oil. Coconut oil can withstand high temperatures and will not burn.

4. Once you treat your bread pan, place it down into the slow cooker, on top of the foil balls, and turn the slow cooker on and up to HIGH. This will allow it to preheat – just as you do your oven. If you wish, you can place your loaf pan down into the slow cooker, onto the foil balls, before you fill with the batter or wait until the pan is filled. Be sure to use hand protection if you wait until after it is filled so you do not get burned if you touch the sides of the slow cooker.

5. While each slow cooker is different, it will take about 2 hours for your loaf to cook completely. Test the center for doneness using a toothpick or cake tester.

6. When cooking these recipes, **be sure you turn the lid slightly crooked so steam can escape,** or prop your lid open with a couple of toothpicks. You do not want the condensation that normally forms on the lid to fall into your loaf.

7. Once your loaf is thoroughly cooked, allow it to sit in the pan for 15 minutes, and then carefully dump it out onto a cooling rack.

8. Once it is thoroughly cooled, which takes about another 30 minutes to an hour, you can slice yourself a piece and feast on the flavor. (Can you tell I like nuts?)

Let this be the start of some wonderful baking at your house as you experiment and try new gluten-free breads in your slow cooker!

So, without any further adieu, I present to you **_gluten-free-style quick breads and muffins!_**

Apple Cinnamon Bread

Ingredients:

- 3 eggs, (bring to room temperature)
- 1/4 cup coconut oil, melted
- 2 tablespoons raw honey or pure maple syrup
- ¼ cup unsweetened apple sauce
- 3 tablespoons coconut flour
- 1 cup almond flour
- 1 heaping tablespoon cinnamon
- 1/2 teaspoon baking soda
- ½ teaspoon sea salt
- 1 large, tart apple, peeled, cored and diced

Directions:

1. Turn on your slow cooker to HIGH while you get your ingredients ready
2. Spray or apply coconut oil to the sides and bottom of your loaf pan
3. In a blender, put the eggs, coconut oil, honey, and apple sauce
4. Allow the blender to run on low or medium while you mix up the dry ingredients in a bowl
5. Place the apple pieces in the dry ingredients and coat them with the flour, etc.
6. Pour the ingredients in the blender into the dry ingredients and mix thoroughly
7. Pour the batter into the loaf pan
8. Place the lid on your slow cooker, using a couple of toothpicks to prop it up to reduce any condensation
9. Cook on HIGH for 2 hours
10. Using a toothpick, check for doneness

11. Remove from the slow cooker and place the pan on a cooling rack for 15 minutes

12. Using a knife, scrape the sides loose and gently invert the bread pan so the loaf is on the cooling rack

13. Allow to cool completely

14. Slice and butter if desired

Zucchini and Carrot Bread

Ingredients:

- 2 large eggs (room temperature)
- ¼ cup raw honey or pure maple syrup
- ¼ cup coconut oil
- 1 teaspoon of pure vanilla extract
- 1 tablespoon of coconut flour
- 2 cups almond flour
- 1 tablespoon ground cinnamon
- ½ teaspoon of baking soda
- ½ teaspoon of sea salt
- 1 carrot, grated (1/2 cup)
- 1 zucchini, grated (3/4 cup)
- ¼ cup raisins

Directions:

1. Turn on your slow cooker to HIGH while you get your ingredients ready
2. Spray or apply coconut oil to the sides and bottom of your loaf pan
3. In a blender, put the eggs, honey, oil, and vanilla
4. Allow the blender to run on low or medium while you mix up the dry ingredients in a bowl
5. Add the wet ingredients into the dry ingredients and mix thoroughly
6. Stir in the carrot, zucchini, and raisins
7. Pour the batter into the loaf pan
8. Place the lid on your slow cooker, using a couple of toothpicks to prop it up to reduce any condensation

9. Cook on HIGH for 2 hours

10. Using a toothpick, check for doneness

11. Remove from the slow cooker and place the pan on a cooling rack for 15 minutes

12. Using a knife, scrape the sides loose and gently invert the bread pan so the loaf is on the cooling rack

13. Allow to cool completely

14. Slice and butter if desired

Banana Bread

Ingredients:

- 6 eggs
- ⅓ cup raw honey
- ⅓ cup coconut oil
- 2 ripe bananas
- 1 tablespoon pure vanilla extract
- ½ cup coconut flour
- 1 teaspoon baking soda
- ½ teaspoon salt
- 1 cup of your favorite nuts, chopped (optional)

Directions:

- Turn your slow cooker on HIGH while you prepare your bread recipe and place a rack or 4 small foil balls in the bottom of your cooker
- In a blender, place the eggs, honey, coconut oil, bananas, and vanilla
- Blend until all ingredients are thoroughly mixed
- In a medium bowl, thoroughly combine the flour, baking soda, salt and nuts
- Pour the banana mixture into the dry ingredients and stir until dry ingredients are wet
- Generously grease your loaf pan
- Pour the batter into the pan and place the pan inside the cooker
- Prop the lid open slightly so condensation can escape
- Cook on HIGH for at least 2 hours
- Test for doneness and cook longer if necessary
- When finished cooking, remove from the cooker and allow to set for about 15 minutes

- Gently dump the bread on to a cooling rack

- Cut when ready!

If you want to make muffins instead, you will have to use your oven.

- Preheat oven to 350 degrees

- Follow the instructions as stated above, but pour the batter into greased muffin tins

- Bake 20-25 minutes

Makes 12 muffins

Cranberry Bread

Ingredients:

- 6 eggs (room temperature)
- 1/3 cup raw honey
- 4 tablespoons butter
- 2 teaspoons pure vanilla extract
- 1/2 cup coconut flour
- 1/2 teaspoon sea salt
- 1/2 teaspoon baking powder
- 1½ teaspoons cinnamon
- 1 cup cranberries, thawed if frozen

Directions:

1. Turn on your slow cooker to HIGH while you get your ingredients ready
2. Spray or apply coconut oil to the sides and bottom of your loaf pan
3. In a blender, put the eggs, honey, butter, and vanilla
4. Allow the blender to run on low or medium while you mix up the dry ingredients in a bowl
5. Add the wet ingredients into the dry ingredients and mix thoroughly
6. Stir in the cranberries
7. Pour the batter into the loaf pan
8. Place the lid on your slow cooker, using a couple of toothpicks to prop it up to reduce any condensation
9. Cook on HIGH for 2 hours
10. Using a toothpick, check for doneness
11. Remove from the slow cooker and place the pan on a cooling rack for 15 minutes

12. Using a knife, scrape the sides loose and gently invert the bread pan so the loaf is on the cooling rack
13. Allow to cool completely
14. Slice and butter if desired

Pumpkin Bread

Ingredients:

- 6 eggs
- ⅓ cup raw honey
- ⅓ cup coconut oil
- 2 ripe bananas
- ½ cup canned pumpkin
- 1 teaspoon pure vanilla extract
- ¾ cup coconut flour
- 1 teaspoon baking soda
- ½ teaspoon salt
- 1 teaspoon ground cinnamon
- ½ teaspoon ground nutmeg
- ⅛ teaspoon ground ginger
- 1 cup of your favorite nuts, chopped (optional)

Directions:

1. Turn your slow cooker on HIGH while you prepare your bread recipe and place a rack or 4 small foil balls in the bottom of your cooker
2. In a blender, place the eggs, honey, coconut oil, bananas, pumpkin, and vanilla
3. Blend until all ingredients are thoroughly mixed
4. In a medium bowl, thoroughly combine the flour, baking soda, salt, cinnamon, nutmeg, ginger and nuts
5. Pour the wet mixture into the dry ingredients and stir until dry ingredients are wet
6. Generously grease your loaf pan
7. Pour the batter into the pan and place the pan inside the cooker

8. Prop the lid open slightly so condensation can escape

9. Cook on HIGH for at least 2 hours

10. Test for doneness and cook longer if necessary

11. When finished cooking, remove from the cooker and allow to set for about 15 minutes

12. Gently dump the bread on to a cooling rack

13. Cut when ready!

If you want to make muffins instead, you will have to use your oven.

1. Preheat oven to 350 degrees

2. Follow the instructions as stated above, but pour the batter into greased muffin tins

3. Bake 25–30 minutes

Makes 12 to 15 muffins

About the Author

Amelia Simons is a food enthusiast, wife, and mother of five. Frustrated with traditional dieting advice and trying to discover why she would experience symptoms like headaches and bloating after eating, she came to understand that she had problems tolerating gluten. While researching and learning all she could about this condition, she created alternative ways to fix the foods she and her family had always enjoyed.

Along the way, she shared with others about the symptoms and solutions of gluten sensitivity and intolerance and helped others learn how to change their foods and cooking methods.

As she continued to study about gluten-free eating, she stumbled upon the Paleolithic diet and lifestyle of eating without grains and has never looked back. Without bothering to count calories or stress about endless hours of exercise, eating the Paleolithic way has enabled Amelia and her husband to effortlessly drop pounds and lower their cholesterol.

Although Amelia now enjoys sharing the Paleolithic philosophy with friends and readers, she has been encouraged by friends and family to share what she experiences and has learned about gluten-free eating. Her life experiences now make it possible for you to enjoy favorite recipes that she has transformed into healthy gluten-free dishes.

Acknowledgements

Many thanks to the following photographers from Flickr.com:

- Dan4th
- Whatsername?
- EraPhernalia Vintage
- Joelk75
- Rhea C.
- avlxyz
- busbeytheelder
- NatalieMaynor
- Todd Kravos
- Scarygami
- Patrick Hoesly

Other Books by Amelia Simons

Paleolithic Slow Cooker: Simple and Healthy Gluten-Free Recipes

Paleolithic Slow Cooker Soups and Stews: Healthy Family

Gluten-Free Recipes

Going Paleo: A Quick Start Guide for a Gluten-Free Diet

4 Weeks of Fabulous Paleolithic Breakfasts

4 MORE Weeks of Fabulous Paleolithic Breakfasts

4 Weeks of Fabulous Paleolithic Lunches

4 Weeks of Fabulous Paleolithic Dinners

The Ultimate Paleolithic Collection

Made in the USA
San Bernardino, CA
10 November 2014